I LOVE ME
I LOVE YOU
GUIDEBOOK

SPIRITUAL MEANINGS OF THE
CHARACTERS AND THEIR LIFE LESSONS

BY ANNE PRYOR, M.A.

This children's book was inspired by messages I received from my mother after she passed away. She asked me to share with all children the truth that they are born pure, filled with light and love, and have no original sin. Her wish is for every child to know they are perfect just as they are.

Devin: The Child of Light

SPIRITUAL MEANING:

Devin represents the innate purity, goodness, and spiritual light present in every child. He is a symbol of the soul's original wholeness-born perfect, loving, and worthy, needing nothing to earn love or acceptance.

LIFE LESSON:

You are born with light and love inside you. You do not need to earn your worth. Remembering your true nature helps you stay joyful and kind, no matter what happens.

AUTHOR'S NOTE:

The name **Devin** carries the meaning "divine" or "godlike" in French and Latin, and "poet" or "bard" in Irish and Celtic traditions.

For this story, Devin is interpreted as "the Divine Within," symbolizing the spark of divinity and goodness that lives inside every person. Devin's character was inspired by a neighbor boy with autism. His presence in the story honors the importance of authentic, positive representation of neurodiversity in children's literature, and celebrates the unique light and perspective that autistic individuals bring to the world.

The braces Devin wears are a tribute to my father, Paul, who wore braces like these from age 65 to 93. Despite the challenges, he never complained, embodying resilience, quiet strength, and acceptance. The braces in the story remind us that everyone carries their own challenges, and that courage and grace can shine through in how we live with them.

The Frog: Rules, Fear, and Transformation

SPIRITUAL MEANING:

The frog is a symbol of transformation, caution, and the burdens of external expectations. In many cultures, frogs represent spiritual rebirth and the transition from one state to another. In the story, the frog's rocks and rules symbolize the weight of beliefs, fear, and the pressure to conform, which can dim our inner light.

LIFE LESSON:

Carrying the heavy "rocks" of others' expectations, strict rules, and fear can make us forget our true selves. True safety and goodness come from within, not from blindly following external rules. Letting go of unnecessary burdens allows your light to shine.

AUTHOR'S NOTE:

In this story, Mr. Frog is a symbol for the Catholic Church's teachings, especially its focus on dogma and manufactured rules. This book was inspired directly by after-death communications (ADC) from my mother, who passed away in March 2025.

My mother struggled deeply with loving herself. She grew up

believing she was "unclean" because of the doctrine of original sin-a teaching in Catholicism that says all humans are born with a spiritual stain inherited from Adam and Eve. This belief, along with other strict rules of the Church, led her to develop obsessive-compulsive behaviors, like constant hand washing and frequent confession, always feeling she needed to be cleansed or forgiven.

Sadly, these teachings also made it hard for my mother to fully accept and embrace me, especially because of my sexuality. The idea that we are born "sinful" or "flawed" weighed on her heart and affected our relationship.

After her passing, my mother reached out to me in spirit. She apologized for the pain caused by her beliefs and told me that I am perfect just as I am. She shared that she had been misled by the Church's teachings and wanted all children to know the truth:

You are not born unclean. You are not broken. You are perfect, lovable, and worthy just the way you are.

This book is her message of healing and freedom for every child and family: Let go of heavy beliefs that make you feel less than whole. Embrace your light, your love, and your true self. You are perfect, just as you are.

Happie Hummingbird: Joy, Lightness, and Resilience

SPIRITUAL MEANING:

The hummingbird is a messenger of joy, beauty, and the connection between the physical and spiritual worlds. It teaches us to find delight in the present, to be agile and adaptable, and to seek the sweetness in life's moments.

LIFE LESSON:

- Find joy in simple things and savor the sweetness of life.

- Be light-hearted and resilient, even when facing challenges.

- Small acts of love and kindness matter.

- Embrace change, adapt, and trust your ability to rise above difficulties.

Boldy the Blue Butterfly: Authenticity and Spiritual Renewal

SPIRITUAL MEANING:

The butterfly is a universal symbol of spiritual renewal, transformation, and the beauty of being yourself. Its journey from caterpillar to butterfly mirrors our own spiritual growth and the courage to show our true colors.

LIFE LESSON:

- Be yourself and let your unique light shine, without worrying about others' opinions.

- Embrace change and transformation as natural and beautiful.

- Authenticity brings joy to you and those around you.

- Everyone's "dance" is special, and the world is brighter when we are true to ourselves.

AUTHOR'S NOTE:

My mom and I shared a special promise: she would return to me as a blue butterfly. This part of the story holds deep meaning for me, because throughout her life, my mom struggled with the belief that I was "unclean." The lesson of the blue butterfly is especially important, as it symbolizes her transformation and her message of unconditional love and acceptance. Through Boldy the Blue Butterfly, my mom reminds me-and all children-that we are beautiful, whole, and perfect just as we are.

Wiggly the Worm:
Forgiveness, Humility, and Renewal

SPIRITUAL MEANING:

Worms symbolize humility, renewal, and the power of transformation through forgiveness. They turn old, decaying matter into fertile soil, representing the ability to transform pain and mistakes into new growth.

LIFE LESSON:

- Forgive yourself and others to heal and grow.

- Let go of anger and hurt, turning them into fresh starts.

- Mistakes and wounds can lead to renewal and greater kindness.

- True strength is in humility and the quiet work of helping others flourish.

AUTHOR'S NOTE:

After my mom passed away, I had to learn how to forgive her for the way she treated me during her life. Through after-death communication, she reached out to me and expressed deep sorrow for her actions. She explained that she had been lied to, tricked, and taught falsehoods by the church about people's differences. My mom asked for my forgiveness, and I was able to offer it to her willingly and lovingly. This experience brought healing to both of us, and it is my hope that sharing our story will help others find understanding, compassion, and forgiveness in their own lives.

Queen Bella Bee:
Love, Teamwork, and Trust

SPIRITUAL MEANING:

The bee represents community, harmony, and the sweetness of shared love and purpose. Bees work together in perfect trust, each contributing to the well-being of the hive.

LIFE LESSON:

- Love and teamwork create a joyful, harmonious life.

- Trust and cooperation are more powerful than strict rules or fear.

- Sharing and helping others brings abundance and happiness.

- True belonging comes from lifting each other up, not weighing each other down.

AUTHOR'S NOTE:

My mom often used the image of a Queen Bee and her hive to describe what the spirit world is like. She believed that the Divine Source-God-is like the loving Queen Bee, watching over all the bees in the hive. Each bee is equally loved, valued, and perfect, just as we are all cherished and cared for by the Divine.

Connecting to Life's Lessons

Each character in Devin's journey offers a spiritual lesson for children and adults alike:

- **Devin** teaches us to remember our original goodness and self-love.

- **The Frog** warns against letting fear and rigid rules overshadow our innate inner Divine light.

- **Happie Hummingbird** inspires us to find joy, adapt, and spread kindness.

- **Boldy the Blue Butterfly** encourages us to be authentic and not worry about others' opinions.

- **Wiggly the Worm** shows the power of forgiveness and renewal.

- **Queen Bella Bee** reminds us that love, teamwork, and trust create true happiness.

Together, these characters guide us to a life of light, love, freedom, and spiritual wholeness.

Summary Table

Character	Spiritual Meaning	Life Lesson
Devin	Innate purity, light, and love	You are born good and worthy; remember your true self.
Frog	Transformation, caution, burden of rules	Let go of fear and others' expectations to find your light.
Happie Hummingbird	Joy, beauty, resilience, spiritual messenger	Find joy in the present, be adaptable, and let love guide you.
Boldy Butterfly	Authenticity, spiritual renewal, transformation	Be yourself, embrace change, and let your true colors shine.
Wiggly the Worm	Forgiveness, humility, renewal	Forgive, grow from hurt, and help others through kindness.
Queen Bella Bee	Love, teamwork, trust, community	Work together, sharing, and trust-true love is joyful and free.

Reflective Questions for Connecting to Life's Lessons

Devin: Remembering Our Original Goodness and Self-Love

- What are some things you love about yourself, just as you are?

- Can you remember a time when you felt proud or happy simply for being yourself?

- How can you remind yourself each day that you are already good and lovable?

The Frog: Letting Go of Fear and Rigid Rules

- Are there any rules or worries that sometimes make you feel heavy or less happy?

- When do you feel afraid to be yourself, and what helps you feel safe again?

- What rocks can you let go of?

Happie Hummingbird:
Finding Joy, Adapting, and Spreading Kindness

- What are some little things that bring you joy every day?
- How do you bounce back or find happiness when something doesn't go your way?
- What is one kind thing you can do for someone else today to help their heart feel lighter?

Boldy the Blue Butterfly:
Being Authentic and Not Worrying About Others' Opinions

- When was a time you did something your own unique way, even if it was different from others?

- How does it feel when you try to be like someone else instead of being yourself?

- What helps you feel brave enough to show your true colors?

Wiggly the Worm: Forgiveness and Renewal

- Has anyone ever hurt your feelings, and how did you move forward?

- Why do you think forgiving someone (or yourself) can help you feel lighter and happier?

- Can you think of a time when you made a mistake but learned something good from it?

Queen Bella Bee: Love, Teamwork, and Trust

- What does it feel like to work together with others on a team or in your family?

- How do you show love and trust to the people around you?

- Can you think of a time when helping someone else made you feel happy inside?

These questions are designed to spark meaningful conversations between children and families, helping everyone reflect on their own journey toward light, love, and wholeness.

Anne Pryor, M.A., is a children's book author and the creator of Lovitude™, and a Soul Painter. This art form fuses love and gratitude-energies she believes are the highest in the universe. Using alcohol ink, her breath, and essential oils on plastic, Anne has created over 7,000 "visual blessings," celebrated for their ability to awaken souls and transform their pain into love. Her vibrant artwork has been featured worldwide, including at the Mayo Clinic, and is licensed on products distributed globally.

Anne's journey as an artist began unexpectedly after she received profound after-death communications from her late mother and a close friend. These spiritual encounters inspired her to create soul paintings and, more recently, to write a children book. Her stories are rooted in the message she received from her mother: that every child is born perfect, without original sin-a message of inherent goodness and divine connection that she now shares.

Before embracing her calling as a Soul Painter and author, Anne was a successful corporate executive, holding marketing leadership roles at Valleyfair, Lifetouch, Carlson Marketing, and as the first employee to open Mall of America's Knott's Camp Snoopy, where she collaborated with Charles Schulz's team. Drawing on her business acumen, Anne became a renowned LinkedIn strategist and executive coach, helping leaders and organizations cultivate authentic connections and meaningful online presence.

Anne holds a Master's Degree in Human Development and Holistic Health and Wellness, and her philosophy of interconnectedness and purpose infuses both her art and her coaching. She is a sought-after speaker, recognized for her work in authentic leadership, heart-centered business, and the transformative power of love and gratitude.

Now residing near Hutchinson, Minnesota, Anne continues to inspire through her Lovitude art, keynote presentations, and children's books. She invites everyone to remember their soul's purpose, embrace their innate goodness, and recognize that we are all connected, here to do our highest good.

Connect with Anne Pryor on LinkedIn to explore her art, books, and insights.

Made in the USA
Monee, IL
03 June 2025